BREAK OUT

by

HERBERT BROKERING

Illustrations by

JIM COLLINS

Concordia Publishing House
Saint Louis   London

Published by
Concordia Publishing House, St. Louis, Missouri
Concordia Publishing House Ltd., London, E. C. 1
Copyright © 1970 Walther League
Library of Congress Catalog Card No. 76-112686
MANUFACTURED IN THE UNITED STATES OF AMERICA

MEANING OF *BREAK OUT*

THIS IS DIALOG on the inside of events. It is an inside look of the outside. It is the interior—the seed—the inner—the heart of the matter—the dynamic—the power from within—the opening up—the breaking down—the breaking out.

Each title is a clue. No more. No less. It is a way in and out of the vignette. It is a suggestion. Every reader creates his or her own title. The title is a way to say it— hear it—feel it—understand it—mean it—believe it.

The basis is in the Christian power to break out. It is the power of the resurrection of Christ, and all the manifestations of this power. It is the power over imprisonment, in life and in death. "Born in a Box" is the theological clue to the book. Read it first—and last—and as the refrain to each. So the special type set for "Born in a Box." On the count of three He arose. In the fullness of time He came. In every fullness of time He can come, bring to life, He can raise up, and He can cause life to break out.

We can plunder or celebrate. We can surrender or win. This book is a declaration of faith that Christ came that we might celebrate and win. That we might know the power of the Gospel from within. We are not imprisoned forever. Perhaps for a night, a year, or a week—but not forever. We celebrate where some only mourn. We live where some only die. We win where some only lose.

Break out. It is Easter; it is Christmas; it is Pentecost in the box. In whatever box.

It is into the world that He came, and the miracle of His coming and daily presence is in the midst of every imaginable box. He gives life in what without Him would be death.

Break out in me, O Christ. Be born again in my box, and make me a Bethlehem. Amen!

Break Out can be used . . .

. . . by adults with youth — youth with youth — youth with adults . . .

. . . to raise some questions — open imagination — begin conversation — lead into devotion — stimulate meditation — focus discussion . . . .

. . . and read — discussed — painted — performed — argued — prayed — done — read antiphonally — dramatized — pantomimed — spoken in choric union — pondered — continued . . .

Contents

Meaning of Break Out	5
Born in a Box	9
Dance Out	13
Cry, Baby	16
Unscrew the Lid	20
Begin Again	23
Plant All Property Lines	26
Old, Be New	29
Wait for Love	32
Say the Right Word	36
Use All Colors	39
Have a Heart	42
Word, Come Back	45
Junk, Arise	49
Open for Peace	53
See the Scene	56
Prison, Be Opened	59
Lord of Labs and Altars	62
Love in Motion	66
Tell When It Hurts	69
Break the Grief	72
Beyond Words	75
The Spirit of the Letter	78
Make the Speeches Dance	81
Laugh It Through	84
A School Cry	88
She Needed a Question	91

Dance Out

It was a fading train depot.
Even the depot pews creaked
with boredom. The boy and
girl saved the late night.

Some dance; some plunder.
Some dance right out of boxes.

The two were alone.
A BOY AND A GIRL.
Hunting birds in the evergreen.
STUFFED BIRDS IN THE EVERGREEN.
By the waterfall.
THE TINY PLASTIC WATERFALL BY THE EVERGREEN.
In the train depot.
A PLASTIC TURQUOISE WATERFALL
AND STUFFED BIRDS.
The water was real.
THE EVERGREEN WAS REAL.
The children were real. And so was the hunt
for the birds.
A BOY AND A GIRL,
HUNTING BIRDS IN THE DEPOT BEFORE SUNRISE,
SNEAKING UP ON THE BIRDS,
ON THEIR TIPTOES, LOOKING, PEEKING.
Looking long into the branches
and glancing quickly.
Counting cloth birds,
smiling, dancing, whirling, counting,
hunting.
THEY NEVER SAW THE CROWDS
MILLING TO THE TICKET WINDOWS.
They marveled at the
plastic waterfall and the plastic holly.
PLAYING HIDE-AND-SEEK WITH CLOTH BIRDS
AND WITH EACH OTHER.
The depot was the stage.
THE TURQUOISE WATERFALL THE STAGING,

AND THEY WERE ALIVE.
Live. Flitting, unconsciously, darting.
TWITTERING.
And startled.
They stood startled in their tracks.
LIKE FROZEN BIRDS.
Like stuffed birds.
STARTLED BY THE LOUD RUNNING
OF TWO CHILDREN, TWO OTHER CHILDREN.
Plundering the waterfall,
and a mother screaming, "Get out!
Don't run! Quiet! Shut up!"
IT RIFLED THROUGH THE DEPOT LIKE
HUNTING SEASON ON BIRDS.
And the two on tiptoe stood on
their flat feet.
FRIGHTENED FOR AWHILE.
Startled by the sudden ravaging
of the turquoise falls.
And by the raping of the evergreens.
THEY WERE AFRAID AS LIVE BIRDS. FRIGHTENED
BY THE SLAMMING OF THE DOOR.
They froze. They walked away
and watched from a distance
until the plunderers moved on.
TO THE GUM MACHINE.
TO PILLAGE ANOTHER SACRED PLACE
IN THE DEPOT.
THEY WAITED, AND THEY RETURNED.
The two on tiptoe peeking
and skipping a circle around the tree.
AND STARING AT THE PLASTIC GREEN HOLLY
AND POINTING AT THE RED BIRDS
AND COUNTING COTTON BIRDS.
Unconscious
of the echo of the gum machine.

Thank You, my Lord,
for the children. The little ones.
Those who tell how it really is.
Those who are still honest.
Those not yet phony.
Thanks for the little children.   *Amen.*

Cry, Baby

There was a five-hour layover. Sometimes there is nothing to do but watch the people and imagine the ceremony going on in the minds of those waiting at the gates. There was this family. The rest could have been.

The baby opened the box. It cried.

They all came.
IT SEEMED LIKE ALL.
The women.
The father. Grandfather.
AND THE BABY.
She held the baby to her.
AND TO THE WINDOW.
They looked through the smoked glass.
AT NIGHT.
The loudspeaker announced the arrival.
THEY MOVED TO THE CORRIDOR.
But they did not go down the concourse to Gate 7.
The long concourse.
THEY WAITED.
As though not to rush him.
To let him come on his own.
AT HIS OWN SPEED.
He was coming.
THAT'S WHAT SHE SAID, GLAD AND AFRAID.
HE'S COMING.
They did not run. They stood in silent restraint.
APPREHENSION.
Tension.
AS THOUGH NOT SURE HOW IT WOULD TURN OUT.
He kept coming to her.
To his sister.

OR WIFE.
The other held the baby.
THE ONE IN BLUE WAS READY TO HUG THE MAN.
THERE WAS NOTHING BETWEEN THEM.
Nothing.
Not even the baby.
HE WAS IN FRONT OF HER.
In khaki.
HE LOOKED PAST HER.
IT WAS A LOOK MANY MONTHS LONG.
As if to reclaim her slowly.
GRADUALLY.
AFTER A LONG TIME APART.
Away.
HE LEANED ON HER, SOBBING.
He had not hugged her.
SOBBING, AND STARING PAST HER.
Crying his way back.
SOBBING INTO HER SHOULDER.
Remembering his way back.
REPENTING.
Reclaiming her.
And the new baby.
HE HAD NOT SEEN THE BABY.
She had written.
HIS EYES SWAM,
LOOKING HARD AT THE CHILD.
He had not made up his mind about the child.
IT GOT TO HIM.
He reached for it.
He reached his way back.
TO THE BABY.
To the baby and the woman.
HE HELD IT TIGHT.
Smiling.
A LITTLE.
Reclaiming woman and child.
HUGGING THEM.
A lot.
HUGGING HIS WAY BACK.
The baby cried.

A LITTLE.
Already he missed the cry of his buddies
in the familiar bunkers.
HE FELT LIKE A NOVICE WITH THE CHILD.
He'd been famous in the front lines.
Famous for his nerve. For controlling emotions.
AND LEADING MEN THROUGH FIRE AND DEATH.
The baby restored his fame.
IT CRIED.
The crying brought out the hero.
THE CRY RECLAIMED HIM.
Crying his way back.

Reunite the millions
separated by wars of all kinds,
homemade wars and national wars.
Release the emotions of warriors.
Open up deep places,
so they can cry out.
Use tears to bring back joy,
and release even the children
to restore humanness.
Release our feelings,
and bring us to our senses,
Spirit of God.
Amen.

Unscrew the Lid

**It was night. Time to
straighten up the toys.
Why the fuss? What were
the children really telling
their mother?**

**Not everything can live in a box.
Not even toys.**

IT'S BEDTIME.
The best time.
THE WORST TIME.
Bedtime. Time to take down the tower.
THE TINKER-TOY TOWER.
Time to take apart the merry-go-round
before it was done.
DONE BEING PUT TOGETHER
AND BEING WHIRLED UP AND SPUN.
It was a long day on the merry-go-round.
A LONG DAY OF EXPECTATION.
Piece by piece it fell into place.
And now it was night.
AND IT ALL FELL APART.
FOR THE SAKE OF THE HOUR,
THE HOUR FOR BED.
Bedtime.
AND THE HOPE OF THE MERRY-GO-ROUND ENDED.
The day ended.
It was dark.
TIME TO STOP.
Time to clean up.
TEAR DOWN.
Time to clean up.
TEAR APART.
Time to clean up.
TO BRING TO AN END.
To end what was not done.
TO PUT THE PROJECT AWAY.

In a box.
TO LAY THE BLOCKS ON A PILE
AND TO SHUT THE LID.
To take down the beams.
To unfold the engines.
TO TOPPLE THE ANTENNA TOWERS.
To crush the cement wall.
TO HEAP THE BLOCKS INTO A PILE.
A NEAT PILE OF BLOCKS.
To collapse the coliseum.
And the planned bleachers.
TO STOP.
To put it away.
TO START OVER.
OVER AND OVER.
To stop.
AT BEDTIME.
Bedtime.
TIME TO GO TO BED.
Tear down, put away,
clean up, and go to bed.
GOOD NIGHT.
Good-bye, tower.
TINKER-TOY TOWER.
Just put together.
NOW I LAY ME DOWN TO SLEEP.
I PRAY THE LORD THE TOYS TO KEEP.
Good morning.
HERE WE GO AGAIN.
Unscrew the lid.
IT WON'T SCREW ON ANYMORE.

Neatness isn't everything.
Not everything is for boxes
and for organization and rules.
Some things need more time
to happen.
Some people need more time
to become alive.
Lord, show me the boxes
and the rules
that don't fit.
Amen.

Begin Again

Youth concerts are sometimes like rehearsals. This one was always a mixture of excellence and surprise. The surprise was the soloist. A virtuoso from the symphony. He goofed. The kids forgave him. They loved him. He was fallible. He was no phony.

**Surprise is always a way out of the box.
And forgiveness breaks down walls.
Box walls.**

He's a virtuoso.
A GRADUATE OF THE SYMPHONY.
Guest soloist.
THE CHILDREN ARE GLUED TO HIM.
Their black-and-red uniforms are as quiet
as a checkerboard,
and they're like hypnotized.
THE VIOLIN IS LIKE A TOY TO HIM.
He's like a pro, and he couldn't fumble it.
EVEN IF THE WHOLE VIOLIN SECTION
TACKLED HIM.
It's tucked in there tight and free.
And his left fingers slide over the four strings.
THE STRINGS ARE LIKE WAXED,
LIKE AN ICE RINK.
And his fingers do acrobatics
over the surface of the nylon.
They jump on the strings
with the vibrato of a trampoline.
THEY ARE LIMP.
They are trained to jump four octaves
and to send chords and solos into their ears
and into their eyes. It is also what they see.
SEE HIM BEGIN.
Play seven measures, and stop!
A VIRTUOSO STOP—
IN FRONT OF ALL THE CHILDREN.
Stop and start over.

RETUNING THE ONE STRING. EVERYONE LOOKING.
HE JUST QUIT IN THE MIDDLE
OF THE SEVENTH MEASURE.
The string was not right.
IT WAS NOT NOTICEABLE. NO ONE COULD TELL.
It was sharp or flat. It took only ten seconds.
HE'D TAKEN LONG AT THE BEGINNING. TUNING.
TIGHTENING THE PEGS.
He has a sensitive ear.
HE SHOULD HAVE GOTTEN IT RIGHT THEN.
THIS WAS A PERFORMANCE.
His first. They'd only heard of him.
They waited long to hear him.
AND SEE HIM. IT SEEMED MORE
LIKE A REHEARSAL.
STOPPING TO TUNE ON THE VERY FIRST PAGE.
They saw him.
NO ONE MOVED. THEY SEEMED SURPRISED.
Surprised.
THAT HE'D OPEN HIMSELF TO CRITICISM.
They didn't budge when he did it.
NO ONE HAS MOVED FOR FIVE NUMBERS.
Except to applaud. Four numbers, four ovations.
THERE WILL BE A FIFTH.
But they'll remember that he stopped
to tune the violin.
WE'LL ALL REMEMBER.
That the one string wasn't right.
That he stopped to tune it,
that he did it as if it was part of the piece.
THAT HE TUNED IT AND STARTED OVER.
They'll probably bring him back for an encore.
EVEN IF HE STOPS NOW TO RETUNE A STRING.

He was not too proud.
He was like a sinner.
He made a mistake.
They forgave him.
And the sinner became a kind of saint.
Isn't that the way it is,
Jesus?
Amen.

Plant All Property Lines

All the people on the street were new. The street was new. The property lines were set deep in the ground. They were stakes underground. Slowly the neighbors met. They held their encounter on the property lines. For some years these lines were like war lines. In grass mowing they waged war and made peace.

Property lines. Possessions. Economics. Sometimes there are the walls and partitions through which men must break to be brothers.

HOW FAR DO I MOW?
To the property line.
YOU MEAN UP TO THE ROW OF LILAC BUSHES?
No, this side of the row.
BUT HE PLANTED THE LILACS TWO FEET
ON OUR SIDE OF THE PROPERTY LINE.
Before the surveyors came out. He did not know.
HE COULD HAVE WAITED UNTIL
THE PROPERTY-LINE STAKES WERE IN.
IT WAS MIDSUMMER WHEN HE
PLANTED THE BUSHES. THEY ALMOST DIED.
That's when he could get them,
from someone he knew. Free.
AND MAYBE HE WAS IN A HURRY
SO HE COULD GET SOMETHING ELSE FREE.
Free bushes?
NO. TWO FEET OF GROUND
TIMES 117 FEET DEEP FREE.
THAT'S 234 SQUARE FEET OF FREE GROUND.
Between our property.
OF OUR PROPERTY.
He planted the lilacs. Watered them the rest
of the summer. They would have died.
AND THEN, WHEN THEY GROW BIGGER,

AND SPREAD, THEY'LL BE TEN FEET WIDE.
What do you suggest?
THAT WE NOT HAVE THIS HEDGE. JUST A FENCE.
The hedge is here; the hedge is growing. Now What?
SUGGESTION.
PROPERTY LINES BE STRIPS OF LAND,
BETWEEN PROPERTIES,
AND NOT BELONG TO EITHER SIDE.
To either side?
RIGHT!
It would grow into a hedge of weeds.
Who would cut the weeds that didn't belong to anyone?
ALTERNATE SUGGESTION.
PROPERTY LINES BELONG TO BOTH PEOPLE.
You mean to meet mathematically, like in a line?
NO, MORE THAN THAT.
IT'S PROPERTY THAT MERGES
AND BELONGS TO BOTH NEIGHBORS.
How much property?
OH, MAYBE SOMETHING LIKE TWO FEET.
That's what the lilacs are.
GIVE ME THE MOWER.

Christ, You said
fences and walls and partitions
are to break down.
Show us that
where we fight fences
and remove walls
You stand there.
Join us
on all our property lines.
Tell us again
that love begins with the neighbor,
especially the enemy.
Amen.

Old, Be New

What is the new? In his case the new was a careful revival of the old. The discovery of the original.

Even translations can become old. Some people are locked into the very stories of history, in which people found freedom. Every generation translates, or it will end in yesteryear's box.

HE IS THE NEW TEACHER.
The new one.
WITH THE NEW TEACHING.
The new understanding.
THE NEW.
The new information. He says how it happened.
WHY IT HAPPENED.
The story.
THE STORY BEHIND THE STORY.
He tells how it was.
AS IN THE DAYS OF EXILE.
Their God had let them down.
THEY NEEDED A SHOT IN THE ARM.
They sang. The refugees sang old songs
they'd almost forgotten.
THE PSALMS.
They were new ones. Like those of David.
LIKE THE GOOD OLD DAYS. NOTHING LIKE
REMEMBERING THE GOOD TIMES.
The golden age. They clung to their heritage.
They kept dietary laws more than ever.
DANIEL DID.
Patriotic. People reclaiming
what they had taken for granted.
THEY TOLD STORIES. ABOUT GOD,
THE CREATOR.
The stories were courageous.
CRIES OF COURAGE.
God made heaven and earth in the beginning.
THEIR GOD.

Surely He would save them.
THEY WERE SURE. THE STORIES WERE LIKE NEW.
The God who made man, spared Noah,
and began again with Abraham.
THEY WERE GLAD FOR THE STORIES.
We are glad
to know this.
TO KNOW HIM.
Who holds together exile, psalms, David, stories.
We are to know.
WE ARE REFUGEES.
Who sing old songs and retell old stories.
To endure exile.
TO LIVE IN IT.
He teaches new songs.
Old songs like new.
AND THAT THE OLD SONGS WERE NEW
AND OLD STORIES WERE NEW.
Are new
to those in exile.

Why are some so afraid of the new?
You promised us
a new day, new life, new things,
a new earth, a new heaven.
Give more people a respect for the new,
and for the old that can be new.
For the old that is still like new.
Amen.

Wait for Love

Seasons are signs for clocks and calendars. Signs for male and female. Signs for night and morning, death and life, old and new.

Seasons can be boxes.
They can be symbols,
and every box carries a surprise.

The night is long.
LONGER AND LONGER.
The sun sets soon, and the night is long.
LIFE CAN SEEM LONG.
The sun is low.
LOW. LIFE CAN GET LOW.
The wind is brisk. The wind is frozen. Cold.
A THING CAN GET COLD.
The ground is freezing. The trees freeze.
FREEZE.
The breeze can freeze. Breath can freeze.
A GOOD THOUGHT CAN GET COLD.
IT CAN FREEZE.
The water is hard.
YOU CAN WALK ON IT. IT IS STILL AND SOLID.
The wood is hard.
AND BRITTLE.
The snow is deep.
A THOUGHT CAN GET DEEP. IT CAN GET SNOWED.
BURIED.
The night is long.
A NIGHT CAN BE LONG. A MINUTE CAN BE LONG.
The night is dark.
A HEART CAN BE DARK. THE LIGHTS CAN GO OUT.
The ground and hillside is asleep or dead.
ASLEEP OR DEAD. A THOUGHT CAN BE DEAD.
A DEED CAN BE DEAD.
The birds are gone. The branches
creak and watch and wait.
FOR THE BIRDS. A MAN CAN WAIT AND WATCH.

The long night waits and watches for the morning.
A BOY CAN WAIT AND WATCH FOR A MORNING.
FOR A SUNRISE.
The seed waits.
TO RISE.
The roots wait and hope.
A GIRL CAN WAIT AND HOPE.
The sun is higher. It rises sooner.
HIGHER AND SOONER.
The morning comes sooner and sooner.
LIFE CAN RISE.
The night is shorter. Day is longer.
A new season dawns.
A YOUNG MAN CAN HAVE A NEW SEASON.
Ice cracks. It heaves and turns
and churns and breaks loose
like a free man.
LIKE A FREE WOMAN.
It tumbles out to sea. Warm.
A THING CAN BE WARM.
A COLD THING CAN GET WARM.
The crackle and creaking are gone.
The birds have come back.
SINGING. LIFE CAN COME BACK SINGING.
The ground is open.
It can receive the sun and rain and seed.
A MIND CAN OPEN AFTER A LONG HARD SEASON.
The day is long. The sun is high.
THE HEART IS HIGH.
The night will get longer.
AND THE SUN LOWER. AND LIFE WILL BE LOWER.
But the season will end.
The sun will rise higher.
A GIRL CAN RISE.
A boy can rise.

The seasons wait on one another.
So does life.
So do people.
Those who fail wait for forgiveness.
Those who cry wait for lovers.

It is the way You made life, Lord.
And we like it that way.
And we wait on You too.
Amen.

Say the Right Word

A committee can be devastating. For some it is a weapon. For some it is communion.

Words can kill.
Words can make alive.

THERE ARE STACKS OF WORDS.
PILES OF THEM ALL OVER.
All over the desks and tables.
CLOUDING THE WINDOWS.
Smearing the blackboards.
AND CLOGGING THE ERASERS.
Words like litter on the floor.
LIKE POKER CHIPS HEAPED.
Like snow drifted over them.
AND CHOKING IN CONFETTI.
Words and words on the table and floor.
AND SEEPING THROUGH THE RUGS.
Words on their new sweaters and blouses.
LIKE FUZZ THAT WON'T COME OFF.
Words like spilled spaghetti on ties.
STAINING.
No one to remove them. No one able to grab them all.
OR STOP THEM ALL.
No one is able. They are the scraps.
THE LEFTOVER WORDS.
The rejected ones.
THE SENTENCED ONES.
Refused by the resolutions, by ammendments.
BY SUBCOMMITTEES, BY INTERRUPTIONS,
BY RIDICULE.
Refused by those who specialize in shooting down words.
WORD WARFARE.
Like gunning down innocent words.
TRIGGER-HAPPY TONGUES.
Like set for long-range artillery.
LIKE SHORT-RANGE FIRE.
Always ready to fire.

SHE IS COVERED WITH WORDS.
She is groping, like lost.
LOST IN THE PILE
OF HER OWN WORDS. REFUSED.
She is hid under the heap.
SHE IS QUIET NOW.
They have run out of ammunition.
SHE HAS RUN OUT OF WORDS.
The dictionary will not help her.
SHE HAS RUN OUT OF COURAGE.
Courage to say one more thing.
ONE MORE SUGGESTION.
The planning committee has silenced her.
ONE DOWN AND NINE TO GO.
There are ten. Her name is on top of the list.
THE PRINTED LIST OF THE COMMITTEE.
Nine to go.
THERE IS TIME. IT IS ONLY THE FIRST HOUR.
Unless something happens.
AND SHE IS REVIVED.
After the break. The Coke break.
THE FOUNTAIN. THE STRAWS. THE RELIEF.
The chance to stretch. And take a little walk.
AND STAND UP.
And go on.
WILLING TO GO ON. AND PERHAPS
TO START OVER.

Lord, words
are a means of grace to me.
When I get caught in them,
dead and buried in them,
send the Word
that frees me from all the words.
Just say the word
when it must be said.
Amen.

Use All Colors

The news mentioned the plans for a new school. What about the color of the atmosphere? And why not let the students paint?

Boxes come in color. All shades.

Think new.
NEW SCHOOL.
A new push-button panel.
I HAVE IT. TEN BUTTONS
ON A PAINTING BOARD.
Ten colors. Then color buttons.
ON ONE MANUAL.
On the center of the groups. Outside.
AND WIRED TO THE INSIDE. INTO EVERYTHING.
A spectrum of color wired to
the walls and ceilings.
MOUNTED IN PUBLIC.
For the first ten to come.
AFTER SUNRISE.
The first ten after sunrise set the color tone.
THEY CHOOSE THE COLOR.
For the one day.
THE COLOR OF THE LABS ON ONE BUTTON.
Instant color.
TEN SETTING THE COLOR.
DECORATING WITH THEIR FINGERTIP.
The color for the hallways.
ANY OF THE TEN COLORS.
One per day.
TWO FOR THE HALLWAYS.
Those going east and west.
AND SOUTH AND NORTH.
The conference rooms.
THE LOCKERS PROGRAMED TO THE PAINT BOARD.
The cafeteria and the closets.
BOOKCASES AND CHALKBOARDS AND BENCHES.
And the desks.

AND THE LAVATORIES.
The ten colors at sunrise.
THE FIRST TEN IN LINE COLOR THE SCHOOL.
They stand there and do it,
and no one stops them.
THE CITIZENS OF THE SCHOOL DECORATE.
They are the artists. The paint poets.
THEY ARE THE BARBER'S BOY.
The son of the bus driver.
THEY CHOOSE THE SCHOOL COLOR.
The daughter of the custodian.
THE TWINS OF THE BANKER.
The paper boy.
THE LONELY GIRL, HUNTING FOR PURPLE.
The lover. He comes with color.
THE CHILDREN OF THE WAITRESS.
The son of the mechanic on the night shift.
THE POLICEMAN'S ONLY SON,
PAINTING THE SOUTH WING.
The math professor takes his turn,
selecting the yellow for the lockers.
YELLOW LOCKERS ALL DAY UNTIL MORNING.
And the next daily edition
of tone for lockers and labs.
AND THE MOODS. AND PURPLE TURNS GREEN.

Lord, You made color
and gave it to us
to decorate the world.
Give us the spirit
that does not spare paint
in the spaces that need color.
Give the schools their color,
all the colors in the spectrum.
And the mood they stand for.
Give us the ability
to color the mood
of the space we take,
being at school.
Amen.

Have a Heart

Heart transplants had a start. The thought came about the heart. What about the heart of a woman in her lover? Inside her unfaithful lover?

To live in another person's box is what Jesus is all about. He still lives on in women and in men.

SHE IS DEAD.
Upon arrival. Poor woman.
BUT THEY TOOK HER HEART.
Stitching, clamping, sewing it.
Into him.
IT WAS HER WISH.
To give him her heart if he should ever need it.
AS HE DOES NEED IT.
AFTER THE SCARS IN HIS OWN.
His heart was practically gone.
IT WAS PRACTICALLY GONE,
IS WHAT OTHERS SAID.
His heart for her and for the other girl.
HIS HEART WAS NOT ON HER.
NOW HER HEART IS IN HIM.
His heart beat for all the others, it seemed.
Passionately.
AND NOW HER HEART IS IN HIM.
His heart pounded when
he saw her, they said. It was an
angry heart.
NOW THE ANGER WILL BE IN HER HEART,
IN HIM.
And his blood pressure rose as he visited
the whores. He told it after
drinking. He even told her without hesitating.
NOW THE LUST WILL FILL HER HEART IN HIM.
He ran around. The nights were too long.
His heart wore out.
HER HEART WAS LIKE NEW.
HAD IT NOT BEEN FOR THE CRASH,

SHE MIGHT HAVE OUTLIVED HIM BY 20 YEARS.
Now he can outlive her by 20.
AND RUN AROUND, AGAINST HER.
With all the others, with her heart in him.
SHE USED TO CRY. SHE NEVER QUIT
LOVING OR FORGIVING.
Her broken heart is beating in him now.
AND SHE DID NOT QUIT PRAYING
THAT HE MIGHT RETURN.
He will have time to return. He was dying.
THAT IS WHY SHE HURRIED TO SEE HIM.
HE WAS DYING. NOW HE IS LIVING.
He is having another chance.
THERE WERE SO MANY CHANCES.
She never quit.
NOT EVEN NOW. HER HEART IS BEATING STRONG.
He never did have a heart like this.
HE WILL LIVE.
I hope so, doctor.
We will tell him when he is out of danger.
THAT HER HEART IS IN HIM.
He will take care of it.
HER HEART.
WITH HIS OWN LIFE.
If only she knew.
HE ACHED FOR HER TO COME.
THAT IS WHY SHE HURRIED.
If only she knew.
IF ONLY HE KNEW.
He will.

Lord, we live very close.
We people are very close.
And that's the only way to do it.
Keep us people close.
Amen.

Word, Come Back

She said she programed music in the wards for the sick. The men were sick from the war. We talked about the power of remembering the past.

One word can be a whole world.
It can close;
it can open.
One box, one word.

THEY WERE BEGINNING TO READ.
And to remember.
THE MEN AND THE NEW BOOK.
The round book.
BEGINNING IN THE CENTER.
The first word was in the center.
THEY KNEW THE WORD. ONCE.
Everyone knows it.
THE WORD WAS A HEAVY ONE. A LOUD WORD.
It fell on the page with a burst.
IT RIPS AT THE CENTER.
It begins things.
IT IS THE BEGINNING FOR THE MEN.
It catches their eyes. The ears.
IT FALLS ON THE PAGE LIKE A PEBBLE
IN WATER.
Like a stone. A rock.
AND THE WORDS RIPPLE FROM IT.
They circle it. Silent words. Dim words.
Invisible words.
THERE ARE WAVES OF WORDS.
A circumference of words.
AND PHRASES.
CIRCLING. SPIRALING SENTENCES OF WORDS.
Enclosing the word.
OPENING IT UP.
Rounds of words, like rounds of ammunition.
SPIRALS OF WORDS, LIKE BULLETS SPINNING.
Tumbling over one another.

Chasing one another.
Smashing.
AND FINDING THE MEANING OF THE FIRST WORD.
Carrying the force of the first word.
ENLARGING IT. RIPPING IT WIDE OPEN.
Doubling it and tripling it.
MULTIPLYING IT.
On a round page.
LOOKING LIKE GEOMETRY.
Like a compass gone wild. A bullet gone wild.
LIKE A WORD IN ORBIT. WHIRLING.
The men are whirling.
WITH WHIRLING WORDS.
Men on a merry-go-round. Unwinding.
AS IN A WHIRLWIND.
Unwinding.
SPIRALING THEIR WAY BACK.
Creating a circle of words.
THEIR WORDS. THEIR FRIGHTFUL WORDS.
Their own rounds of words and curved categories.
THE ROUND PAGE IS NOW FULL.
IT OPENS UP THEIR MINDS.
Their memories.
THEIR TONGUES.
Locked now for two days.
SINCE THE WORD **FIRE!** RIPPED THE NIGHT AIR.
And sent their whole vocabulary into a spin.
LIKE A YO-YO THEY SPUN TO THE END.
Until the third day now.
THEY HAD HIT THE END. OUT.
And they are returning to the word.
THROUGH THE WORD.
It is one word they all know.
WHICH IS THE ONE WORD
TO BRING BACK THESE MEN,
DAZED FOR DAYS.
The word *FIRE!*
FIRE! WAS THEIR LAST WORD.
It was the first word in the page.
THE CENTER OF THE PAGE.
The page looks like a target page.

THEY ARE APPROACHING THE CENTER.
On this third day.
THEY ARE REMEMBERING THEIR FINAL WORD.
Fire!
THEY ARE READING THEIR WAY BACK.
To the center of the page.
TO THE BEGINNING.

There are the sick.
All the sick, Lord.
Sick deep in their mind,
who wait for the right doctor
to come.
Am I the doctor?
Am I the one with the right word
to heal their disease?
I can speak!
I can hear! Send me!
Amen.

Junk, Arise

The man was filled with imagination. He recalled his childhood. He had invented out of necessity. Now it was a habit.

Handicaps can be horizons.
Boxes can grow seed.

POVERTY.
They never called it that.
DEPRESSION.
They did not use the word.
ENOUGH. JUST ENOUGH OF EVERYTHING.
That's where it must have happened.
IN THAT SIMPLE PLACE.
In a simple time of having
just enough of everything.
HE LEARNED HOW TO MAKE HIS OWN.
By rummaging in the junk.
COLLECTING PIECES TO PUT TOGETHER.
Making toys.
CREATING TOYS.
The junkyard was his bench. His warehouse.
STRAIGHT PIPES, CURVED RODS,
AND RUSTED WHEELS.
His tools were his hands. And his head.
THEY COULD NOT BUY HIM WHAT HE NEEDED.
To play.
THEY COULD NOT BUY IT.
The toys they could not buy he made.
AND THEN SOME.
He put them together like a craftsman.
AT SEVEN HE WAS AN INVENTOR.
At 8 and 9 and 10 years.
A KIND OF CREATOR.
Then it happened.
MORE THINGS TO FIT TOGETHER.
More pieces.
THE FALL. THE BROTHER FELL.

And there were new pieces to fit together.
HE PLAYED WITH THEM LIKE JUNK.
It was going on winter. And winter on spring.
THE HILL WAS HIS BENCH.
IT WAS A CLUTTERED HILL.
Heaped. He sorted. He rummaged.
IN THE NEW MOUND OF EARTH. THE MARKER
WITH THE NEW WORDS OF BIRTH
AND DEATH TYPED.
There were new pieces. Many.
THE BROTHER. THE DIRT. THE FREEZE.
THE THAW. THE GREEN GRASS.
The cement and the slogans carved in marble, and Jesus.
JESUS WAS IN THE BOY'S NEW COLLECTION
OF JUNK.
He had never had a course in art or welding.
OR TOY MACHINE. OR THEOLOGY.
OR IN HANDLING JUNK.
He was making what could not be bought.
IN THE DEPRESSION.
In poverty.
HE STILL SPECIALIZES.
In the art of making something.
VALUABLE.
Out of scraps.
PIECES.
Junk.
RUSTED.
Dead.
AND GREEN.
They say he is rich.
STILL DOING IT.
Putting together things.
AS A HOBBY.
For a living.
HIS SON IS DOING IT WITH A CAR.
He has given it a name.
HEAP OF JUNK. THAT'S THE NAME ON THE DOOR.
It'll really run.
I KNOW.

*You know what it is
to make something out of nothing.
It says in Scripture,
You did it in the beginning,
You did it on Calvary,
You can do it here, Lord.
Do it.
Amen.*

Open for Peace

Peace talks. War talks. For awhile the oil painting seemed to look like very, very long ago. Suddenly — the depot painting looked like last night's news, and the Indian was the ambassador.

War is an old box — with all sides shut.

IT WAS A PAINTING.
Forty feet by fifteen feet of oil painting.
THERE WAS NO MENTION OF IT
IN THE TOURIST MANUAL.
The Chamber of Commerce had no record of it.
IT WAS JUST THERE.
In the train depot.
AN ENORMOUS PAINTING BY SOMEONE.
Someone who had the time to put
so much oil and color on one canvas.
SOMEONE WHO HAD A KNACK
FOR PAINTING INDIANS.
A powwow.
HARVEST MOON POWWOW OF THE BLACKFEET
AND THE KOOTENAI TRIBES.
Montana tribes.
HE PAINTED INDIANS
TO LOOK LIKE A PHOTOGRAPH.
The chiefs stood on the edge of
their sand peninsulas
separated by water.
THEY STOOD AT THE EDGE.
It was their peace table,
their peace platform.
The sand of the peninsulas.
THEIR CHIEFS WERE BEHIND THEM
WITH THE WIGWAMS.
And their loved ones.
THIS WAS THE POWWOW IN THE AUTUMN.
To determine boundaries.
FOR HUNTING AREAS.

To determine where they could gather food.
HOW FAR THEY COULD GO.
It was their ministry of economics.
THIS WAS THE POWWOW OF THE HARVEST MOON.
To determine relations.
TO DISCUSS ALL TRIBAL RELATIONS.
Human relations.
HOW FAR THEY COULD GO
WITH ONE ANOTHER.
Without one another.
IT WAS THEIR MINISTRY OF FOREIGN AFFAIRS.
THEIR MINISTRY OF WAR.
Their ministry of housing.
THEIR MINISTRY OF DOMESTIC AFFAIRS.
The powwow was the congress.
The powwow was the ambassadors.
THE POWWOW WAS THE PEOPLE REPRESENTED
BY THE CHIEFS.
The powwow was under the harvest moon.
The time to decide what to do
with the food harvested.
AND THE HUNGER AHEAD.
THE LONG WINTER
AND THE HUNGER.
They decided
and they feasted and they danced.
THEY DECIDED HOW FAR TO LIVE APART.
And how close together.

Peace is what You sent Christ for.
You've been busy, Jesus.
And the talk goes on.
They end and they begin,
generation after generation,
war after war.
We never run out of wars, Jesus,
and You never run out of peace.
Good. Good for us.
Amen.

See the Scene

Much is relative. Even beauty is relative. Beautiful sights and menus and holes.

Monotony is a box. Repetition can build walls. New people can restore sights that have been lost behind the four walls of monotony.

She seated him at a table facing the window.
I LOOKED TO SEE IF HE WOULD LOOK OUT.
HE WAS LARGE AND LOOKING INTO
THE LARGE MENU.
He had said he did not care where he sat.
TWO MEN CAME BY.
Outside it was wet. A soft rain.
Soft, and the rock sparkled,
and the pine trees were intense
against the white and gray of the sky.
The clouds made the sky and ground
one hazy background in the distance.
THE RAIN HAD DONE IT ALL.
IT COULD HAVE BEEN NORWAY OR IDAHO
OR THE ALPS. IT WAS SPOKANE.
"It's beautiful, isn't it?" she said.
A WAITRESS SAYS SUCH THINGS.
"I don't know how rain can ever be beautiful,"
he snapped.
"BETTER THAN SNOW," SAID HIS COMPANION.
She left the men.
HER RAIN SENTENCE WAS THROWN BACK
SO VIOLENTLY. SHE STAYED
WITH THE SUBJECT OF FOOD.
They sat against the window.
THE PICTURE WINDOW.
Washtubs, appliances, toasters was their topic.
Their paper work was uninterrupted by the scene.
THEIR SCENE WAS IN THE LIST,
THE COLUMNS OF FIGURES, THE BATHTUBS.
The waitress had said it was beautiful.

ONE HAD SAID, "SEAT ME ANYWHERE."
One had said, "How can rain ever be beautiful?"
I WAS ON HER SIDE. I TOLD HER.
I asked, "How about the city in the valley?"
"WE'RE KIND OF IN A HOLE HERE," SHE SAID.
A hole. I knew she was with
the traveling men at the window.
She too had lost the scene.
THEY IN THE RAIN.
She in a hole.
THE MAN IN HIS MENU.
The head waitress told her
the pancake pitchers needed fix-up.
SHE ANSWERED.
It's a shame to let them go to waste
when you can have them fixed.
It's a shame to let them go to waste.
She would save the syrup pitcher.
SHE HAD LOST THE SCENE.

There is so much to see!
There is so much to hear and feel
and taste and touch.
It will take our lifetime, Lord,
and then some.
There's so much!
Take away the ho-hum, Lord.
Amen.

Prison, Be Opened

What is punishment? What is rehabilitation? Why solitary confinement? Why cells and walls? Sin came with fences and walls. Where are the doors and the gates? How can the man who hates and murders the people get back among the people?

Loneliness can be a box. Isolation can be a private cottage on a private island; it can be a prison cell. Some live in cells by choice.

It's hard to believe.
YES.
And he'll get penitentiary for it.
MANY YEARS.
The big one up state.
HE'LL GET A CELL.
Too bad.
HE'LL LIKE BEING ALONE.
ALWAYS WAS A LONER.
A cell.
LIKE THE COTTAGE WE BOUGHT.
THE ONE ROOM WE HAD FOR 22 YEARS.
YOU LIKED IT.
He'll have only one window.
THAT'S WHAT OURS HAD. HE CAN
HANG A CURTAIN OVER IT.
Then it won't just look like one hole in the wall.
I'LL SEW THE CURTAIN MYSELF,
LIKE THE ONE IN THE CABIN.
They may not allow it.
HE CAN PAINT SHUTTERS AROUND IT.
IT'LL LOOK LIKE THE COLONIAL DAYS.
That's when it began.
WE CAN GET HIM A NEW TRANSISTOR,
AND HE CAN LISTEN.
THE WAY HE ALWAYS DOES AT THE CABIN.
In the colonial times it started.
YOU KNOW HE ALWAYS READ THERE

AND HE'D NEVER TALK.
THIS'LL BE HIS COTTAGE. HIS OWN.
I read that solitary cells began then.
It was punishment to be alone.
IT WILL REMIND HIM OF OUR VACATION.
BEING AWAY FROM EVERYONE.
Isolation was a penalty then. It brought remorse.
WE CAN GIVE IT A NAME.
WE'LL DO IT AS A GAME.
THE WAY WE NAMED THE COTTAGE. REMEMBER.
He'll get 20 years.
IT COULD BE WORSE.
Like what?
IF THEY DIDN'T GIVE HIM HIS OWN ROOM.
IF HE HAD TO BE AMONG THE PEOPLE.
Yes.
AND WORK FOR 20 YEARS. WE'LL TELL HIM
IT'S LIKE THE VACATION COTTAGE.
NEW PAIN. HE KNOWS.
THAT'S WHERE I GOT THE IDEA.
What color will the curtains be?

How are we to punish?
How are we to take an enemy,
stop him,
and turn him around to love us?
How are we to get the ones cut off
back into the fellowship?
You come to us in Communion,
Christ.
Amen.

Lord of Labs and Altars

Why all the talk about Genesis 1? If God is Creator, will the scientists outsmart Him? Would God flunk chemistry?

The debate between science and religions has isolated many. It has kept them away from the full meaning of both the lab and the altar. It takes a free spirit to know God is at both.

Don't blow up the place?
NO.
Careful. I know all about these things.
You add that, and we'll all be has-beens.
I KNOW.
Where'd you learn science?
I NEVER STUDIED SCIENCE.
Then what are you doing here in this lab?
There must be a law
protecting the world of science
against amateurs like you.
WATCH.
Watch out. Don't mix that, mister!
I'm getting those tubes ready for life.
ARE YOU A SCIENTIST?
My friends say I am.
THEN WHY DO YOU SAY THAT YOU MIX THINGS
AND MAKE THINGS IN THE LAB?
Technically I don't.
What are you doing? Why'd you come
to interrupt my lab work?
TO SET YOU FREE FROM THE TEST TUBES.
Free?
AND FREE FROM ALL FORMULAE—
ON THE BLACKBOARD AND YET UNWRITTEN.
So.
I COMMISSION YOU TO BE A SCIENTIST.

But I'm getting my Ph. D. next month.
YOU STILL NEED TO BE COMMISSIONED.
I will. Now what?
I COMMISSION YOU TO BE FREE
AND TO DISCOVER A UNIVERSE OF SECRETS.
And I don't have to invent and create?
ONLY FIND AND DISCOVER.
Where all have you been?
TO EVERY SCIENCE LAB.
To Cape Kennedy?
I'VE BEEN THERE. I'VE BEEN TO ALL.
And you commissioned every one?
ONLY THOSE WHO BELIEVED ME.
I believe you. Am I free to find life?
YES, YOU ARE FREE;
IF THERE IS LIFE IN THIS LAB,
YOU MAY FIND IT.
Now what are you doing?
MOVING THE BUNSEN BURNERS.
Where are you taking them?
TO THE ALTAR. THE CHURCH ALTAR.
What will people think?
Bunsen burners for candles.
TO CELEBRATE YOUR FREEDOM.
Will we bring them back?
OF COURSE.
THEN THIS WILL BE YOUR OTHER ALTAR.
This lab table and sink.
YES. YOU MAKE A GOOD MINISTER
IN YOUR LAB APRON.
How long have you been doing this?
ASTRONOMERS CAME ALL THE WAY TO BETHLEHEM
TO SEE ME ONCE.

O God,
what a myriad of miracles
You have stored into space and time!
They work and wait
to be unlocked by us.
Take us
and give us a calling

*into the vast worlds
of animate and inanimate,
of personal and social.
Call us into these places,
and meet us there.
Amen.*

Love in Motion

Who was the girl? Why did she so mail the letter? Stop to think of it, many letters are mailed that way. Thoughtfully. Willfully. Critically.

Communicating can be the box. It can be broken in the honest moment of a letter. A word. Something personal and said that waits then for the next honest moment. The answer.

That's that!
THE MAILBOX LIPS SNAPPED SHUT.
It was on its way.
SHE HURRIED ACROSS THE STREET
TO BEAT THE RED LIGHT.
And her mouth twisted in a tiny smile.
SHE HAD DONE IT.
THE LETTER WAS ON ITS WAY.
There was no way to change it.
IT WAS NOT POSSIBLE TO OPEN THE BOX
OR TO REACH IN.
It was not legal.
IT WAS AGAINST THE LAW TO TAKE IT BACK.
It was now the ruling of the federal government
that the letter go through.
IT WAS THE RULING OF HER MIND.
HER HEART WAS NOT SURE.
She had a feeling of relief, and it was
in the way she ran across the street.
SHE COULD SEE THE LOOK ON HIS FACE,
SHE HAD WAITED LONG TO WRITE;
NOW SHE WOULD WAIT TO HEAR.
It was his turn.
THE RELIEF WAS LIKE THE ROSEBED
BY THE WALK.
Freed from the winter freeze.
SHE HAD SAID HER SENTENCE.
NOW HE MUST SAY HIS.
The conversation was the only one

of its kind in the world.
THE CATEGORY WAS AN OLD ONE.
But this was different.
Absolutely no one had ever had this to say.
IN THIS WAY.
They were the only two of their kind
of the 3 billion people or 5 billion.
MULTIPLIED.
THERE IS NO COUNTING THE COMBINATIONS.
And this was like none of those.
She smiled.
SHE HAD JUST CREATED A SENTENCE.
With a new subject and predicate: "I love you."
WHAT HE'D SAY BACK WOULD BE LIKE
NOTHING EVER SAID BEFORE.
Nor again.
"I LOVE YOU," SHE SAID.
No one had ever said it before.
Not this way.

O Christ,
what would life be without love?
And what would love be
without all the ways to make love!
Think of all the ways You loved.
May we think of all the ways
for us to make love.
Amen.

Tell When It Hurts

I always had a fascination for garbage-truck drivers. Imagine the surprise when the man said, "I haul garbage." That was quite a ride.

Everyone needs a time to tell what's hurting. Boxes have feelings.

I haul garbage.
OH.
From morning till night.
I'VE ALWAYS WANTED TO TALK TO ONE.
And there isn't any part of this city
I don't know.
REALLY.
Name any place.
I'LL TAKE YOUR WORD FOR IT.
I pick it up. I dump it.
I DIDN'T HAVE YOU PEGGED AS A GARBAGE MAN.
I know just who they are.
YOU MEAN THE ADDRESSES?
The people.
YOU MEAN THAT? THE PEOPLE?
I can tell about them. Ask them.
YOU CAN TELL ABOUT THEM.
BY THE STUFF THEY THROW AWAY?
I can tell by how they act.
ACT?
By what they pay me and how they do it.
PAY?
By how they bribe me to take them there.
TO THE DUMP?
I know where to drop them, and the places get to smell.
They stink way out to the curb.
STINK?
And they plop down in the back,
and you can tell the stink
by the perfume on them.
YOU SAID YOU DRIVE GARBAGE?

And sometimes it's so strong you think
it's a brewery truck.
And you stop once or twice
while they heave out the door.
If you don't make it,
you clean out the cab the next hour.
BUT YOU SAID GARBAGE.
I've been driving out of this cabstand for 24 years.
Sometimes I feel like I'm hauling garbage.
SO THAT'S WHAT YOU DO.
And I just dump them. That's what I do.
THIS IS WHERE I GET OUT.
See you again.
THANKS.
Thanks.

What do we do with the despised,
the ugly, the fallen, the outcast?
What do we do with enemies?
What did You do, Jesus?
How do You so love the world, Father?
Amen.

Break the Grief

Some resented the way
he grieved. In the long run
it was not possible to
cast a first stone — for anyone.

Grief can have its box.
It can be loud when
it means to be quiet.

He stood before them.
AND THEY WAITED FOR HIS WORDS.
He was never without words.
NOT EVEN AT THE FUNERAL. HE SPOKE LONG.
And his voice did not break.
NOR WHEN HE SANG.
It was louder than others. Louder than all.
HIS VOICE PIERCED THE CROWDED CHURCH.
And cut through the singing.
LIKE A BULLET.
Like 60.
LIKE THE SPEED OF THE CAR THAT HIT
THE EMBANKMENT.
And took her while she slept.
HIS DAUGHTER. TWENTY.
That was a year ago.
THIS HOUR.
And they waited to see him.
AND TO HEAR HIM.
This was Wednesday; that was Friday.
IT WAS A YEAR TO THE DAY.
The chapel was full of officials.
OFFICERS, CO-WORKERS, COLLEAGUES.
And he raised his voice.
TO KEEP IT FROM BREAKING.
And he underlined his words.
TO KEEP THEM FROM FALLING.
He did not weigh his own words.
HE WAS WITHOUT HIS OWN.

He said he was without words. He quoted.
ABRAHAM LINCOLN HAD SUFFERED.
He read the Lincoln words with passion.
COMPASSION. WITH HOPE.
They were like a psalm.
OF MERCY.
A pleading poem.
THE WORDS WEPT. THEY CRIED OUT;
HE SAID THEM LIKE A READING.
As if trying out for a play.
FOR THE LEAD PART, AND TRYING VERY HARD.
He put more stock in the lines of Lincoln
than in his own.
HE DID NOT TRUST HIS OWN SO MUCH.
Not that day. He really tried out for the part.
SO DID I.
In front of everyone.
AND I.
The part of the fumbling believer.
I READ WITH HIM. SILENTLY.
And he got the part. Surely he did.
I READ ALONG.
A perfect cast.
EVERY WORD WAS MINE.
He surely got the lead.
AND I HIS STAND-IN.
He doubted in front of us.
FOR US.

Break the strength of grief.
The grip of silent grief,
and the power of remorse.
Let us not cast stones
at those who are in pain,
nor tell them how they are to cry.
We all cry, Lord,
in our own way.
And then we feel better
in our own way.
Amen.

Beyond Words

He wanted to talk. The word GOD triggered him. He was trying to get past the letters of a word.

There is play on words that distorts meaning. Words have been known to lose their meaning and have become like empty boxes. To get past the letters and vocabulary to the meaning is like a box with a gift inside.

God.
G-O-D.
God.
I SEE THREE LETTERS.
LIKE ON THREE BLOCKS.
WOODEN BLOCKS.
God.
THREE BLOCKS IN FRONT OF MY EYES.
THREE BLOCKS IN FRONT OF YOUR MOUTH.
G-O-D.
God.
GOD IS NOT A WORD.
God.
A TOY. A GAME.
God.
YOU HAVEN'T TOLD ME ANYTHING.
YOU HAVE ONLY GIVEN ME THREE
LETTERS. ONE WORD. BACKWARDS
IT SPELLS DOG. D-O-G.
God.
YOU JUST STAND THERE REPEATING THE
SAME WORD. GOD. GOD. GOD. LIKE
A TAPE LOOP WITH GOD-GOD-GOD HANG-UP.
God.
GOD ISN'T A WORD. HE'S NOT A SENTENCE,
AN ANTHEM, A POEM. GOD IS NOT A BOOK.
God.
HE IS NOT THE BIBLE. GOD IS
NOT JOHN 3:16.
God.

HE IS NOT WORDS AND WORDS AND WORDS.
HE IS NOT THE WORD *LORD, JEHOVAH,
JESUS, BROTHER, JAVEH, CHRIST.* . . .
God.
GOD CANNOT BE SPELLED.
HE CANNOT BE PUT IN CAPS OR TYPESET.
HE CANNOT BE PRINTED IN BLACK INK
OR OFFSET.
God.
HE IS NOT THESE SYLLABLES,
THESE SIGNS, THESE SYMBOLS.
God.
GOD IS A SPIRIT.
God.
HE IS THE SPIRIT BEHIND THE LETTERS.
God.
THE FIRST WORD THEY SAID;
THE FIRST THING THEY DID.
God.
THE ONE BEFORE THE WORDS.
God.
AFTER THE WORDS.
God.
THE EXPLANATION OF THE WORD.
THE EXPERIENCE OF THE WORD.
God.
THE WORD MADE FLESH.
My God.

God, be God.
Be lord of language,
of sentences,
of words.
Take us all the way,
and come to us all the way.
Let there be no words between us.
Let words unite us.
Lord. Christ. Lord.
Amen.

enville: My fellow members of Parliam
at war. After long and hard fig
, France. Our triumph h   sel
                                   between kerygma and Gos
ime Minister, it is   nguish
e in the world

defghijklmnopqrstuvwxyz

NEATNESS COUNTS

...center arou... Catholic theologians, s
Hofinger, William Reedy, and o... ...erygmatic teaching
...the tonic note in Catholic ...tics. Two book
Doctrine and The Goo... ...e... and Its Pr
...b... the basic them... of such te
why they should. After all, ...ey w... need, and... central
tory in the French and Indian War. If we ha... ...o keep
...won't the colonis... ...enefit more by it than the... ...ay
...ontiac's attac... ...p... ...e western settlers bears out
not?

SO WHAT

o Lor...

DEFGHIJKLMNOPQRST
                                                       ...ent of th
hed the Proclamation of 1763, and they took vigorous acti
...p Act.   The colonists disliked Grenville's
...p Act.

ms: Why not our lands, and everything we possess to ma
...re laid upon us in any shape, and if w... have no legal re
...ssist in making the decision as to wh... ...hey are laid, a...
from free subjects to the miserable s... ...of slaves? Taxa
...ian ...

Hofinger, set forth...
doctrine as adornment around th...

WHY?

l. His words are clear:
then, ...hich St. Paul, as the herald, Keryx, of the ...ngress,
...clai... to fallen humanity is ...one other than that b... ...'s wh
...r.... which constitute th... essential content of th... ...assed,
...g... ...e message must bring the inner nature
...ty ... ...s clear focus as possible. It consi... ...party.
good new... ...f the eternal love of God... ...dressed myself in th
n Son ...as c... ...s to Himself. ...atchet.... We were the
...e. In brief, it is ...he o... hatches, and take out all the
                ...o...d, and we immediately proceeded
...cing and spl... ...ng the chests with our tomaha
...ible t... thoroughly to the ...h...ets of the water. We th
...to our several homes without h...ving any conversation
...taking any measures to discover who were our assoc

ABCDEFGHIJK

he British lion was aroused, and there wer... passed law
...h the colonists. These were called by the... ...ts the
Lutheran pastor, John Peter Muhlenberg... his con...
...language of Holy Writ there is a t

The Spirit of the Letter

He was hung up in perfect grammar and editorial rules. What he'd set out to master now controlled him.

Grammar can corner the creative spirit. It can box. It is possible for grammar to open the spirit.

But they're not blind.
THEY HAVE EYES TO SEE, AND THEY DON'T SEE.
They need glasses?
THEY NEED PRACTICE SEEING.
I've been teaching for years.
MAKING THEIR EYES DIM.
They take notes.
WHICH THEY CANNOT READ.
They write them into notebooks.
THERE IS NOTHING TO SEE.
THE PAGES ARE LIKE PENCIL DRAWINGS.
My words.
INK WORDS.
PICTURES OF INK WORDS AND PENCIL WORDS.
IMPRESSIONISTIC ART.
Outlines.
PICTURES OF OUTLINES AND LINES
AND LISTS AND PARAGRAPHS AND HEADINGS.
I believe in neatness.
THEY HAVE BEEN BLINDED BY THE PAPER.
THE WHITE, GLARING PAPER.
They hand it in. I check it.
THEY WRITE ON THE LINES.
THE OP. CITS. AND FOOTNOTES BLIND THEM.
I teach them rules.
THEY ARE BLINDED BY SPELLING
AND CAN SEE ONLY WHAT THEY SPELL RIGHT.
I teach them grammar.
THE PUNCTUATION AND MARGINS HAVE COVERED
THEIR OPTIC NERVE WITH A GROWTH.
They have perfect margins.
THEY WRITE LETTERS AND CROSS T'S

WITH CAUTION AS IF CROSSING
A STREET BLINDFOLDED.
Neatness gets special credit. They have to be careful.
THEY LEAVE INCH-AND-A-HALF MARGINS
THAT ARE CLEAN.
THEY CANNOT DOODLE AND DRAW PICTURES.
They pay attention to what I say.
It helps their concentration.
THEY CANNOT DOODLE THEIR FLASHES
OF INSIGHT INTO MARGINS.
UNLESS THEY ARE SURE.
First they must learn.
THEY ARE LED ON LINES
AND REWARDED FOR REPETITION.
I want to be sure they hear me.
THEIR EARS GROW BIG, AND THEIR EYES DIM.
I enunciate my words.
THERE IS A REWARD FOR HANDING IT IN TYPED.
Ten points for typing.
AND THEIR EYES ARE TRANSFIXED
ON THE KEYBOARD.
Most of them can type without looking.
THEIR EYES ARE IN THEIR EARS.
THEY CRY FOR KINDERGARTEN
AND FINGER-PAINTING AND DOODLING.
They have to grow up sooner or later.
AND DIE AND RISE AGAIN.
Give up the alphabet. The grammar.
LOOK ON THE WALL.
Graffiti.

O Lord, the spirit.
Give us the spirit.
The feel, the life, the breath,
the warmth, the truth.
Lead us by the Gospel.
Open to us the secret
in the sentence
and the picture in the paragraph.
Amen.

UTMOST

FURTHER MORE

MY FRIENDS IT IS W

AND FURTHER

AND LET ME A

IN CONCL

Make the Speeches Dance

How stiff some people get inside the institution! How hemmed in! How crippled by protocol and customs! Could not a boring lecture turn into an elastic ballet? And get across the message? Get it to you. Into you.

People get into ruts. Lectures and speeches are for some already solid boxes. They wall out everything they are meant to express. Some things lose their spirit in the form of lectures.

She had read the invitation.
INFORMATION CLASS.
She had come to learn. She had come from work.
HE HAD INVITED HER.
It was her first year teaching ballet.
THAT'S WHERE THEY MET.
She had seen him every night. He had a strong body,
and his shoulders were strong.
HIS FEET WERE SWIFT,
AND HE WAS A GOOD PARTNER.
This was his class. He said 50 usually came.
HER CLASSES WERE FOR SEVEN.
Enough for the one table.
SHE HAD NEVER SEEN HIM STAND SO STILL.
For 1 hour they sat. 49 sat on 49 chairs.
50 SAT. SHE CROSSED HER LEGS AND SAT
ON THE FLOOR. NO ONE NOTICED.
She had learned to sit cross-legged.
HER LEGS WERE LIKE RUBBER, SOME SAID.
She sat cross-legged. The floor was her playground.
EVERY MORNING FROM 8 UNTIL 7 AT NIGHT.
The floor was like a meadow and a runway,
like a cloud and like a trampoline.
LIKE VELVET AND SPONGE,
AND HER MUSCLES TURNED THE FLOOR
INTO A PLAYROOM.

Her seven romped on the floor, and
with splits and toe stands and cartwheels
there was no part of them that did not.
THE WOOD FLEXED. IT WAS LIKE THE WALLS
OF A BILLIARD TABLE.
It was to their toes and body
as air to the wings of the sea gull.
IT HELD THEIR MOTIONS.
She sat for 50 minutes.
98 FEET WERE A LOT ON THE FLOOR. FLAT.
They sat, and their feet were flat and quiet.
SHE HAD NEVER SEEN THEM STAND SO LONG.
It was as if he had frozen and
all day his feet followed the words,
and the floor held all his emotions
and interpretations
as a page holds the words.
HE WAS STRAIGHT AND STILL.
For 50 minutes he spoke,
and his body did not move.
AND SHE SAT CROSS-LEGGED
AND DID NOT MOVE.
And 98 feet were flat and did not move.
SHE WORKED AND DANCED.
She came again.
SHE DANCED THE WORDS.
He had agreed.
THE WORDS MOVED HER TOES
AND HER TORSO.
He left the lecture stand.
AS HIS WORDS HAD SHAPED HIS FAITH,
SO NOW THEIR WORDS BECAME FLESH.
The sign says *Chairs For Sale*.
Forty-nine.

We have so many senses, Lord.
So much feeling and rhythm.
When the words fail,
then put us on our feet
to dance and do.
Get us out of only straight rows,
and put us on our toes.
Amen.

Laugh It Through

Laughter is what they needed.
They had lost the joy
of each other
and for themselves.
A clown came to their rescue.

Laughter is power
when released.
When imprisoned,
it feels sorry.

They were all old.
IT SEEMED THEY WERE OLD.
14 going on 40.
EIGHTEEN GOING ON EIGHTY.
20 going on 200.
Two hundred years old.
AT TWENTY.
There was but one thing to do:
Face it.
FACE BEING FOURTEEN AND EIGHTEEN.
Face being themselves.
The preacher had been a clown. Full time.
UNTIL HE STEPPED INTO ANOTHER TENT
ONE NIGHT.
The gospel tent. A revival-meeting tent.
THAT'S WHERE HE LEARNED HIS NEW ACT.
Preacher. Now he's a preacher.
FOR EIGHT YEARS NOW.
He was a clown longer.
HE NEVER QUIT.
They like the 10th of each month.
THE YOUNG LIKE IT MOST.
THE YOUNG GOING ON OLD.
And the old never get young.
HE CALLS IT RESURRECTION NIGHT.
They call it hide-and-seek.
THEY HAD TO REBUILD THE VESTIBULE.

CLOSETS.
Closets and drawers for a thousand masks
and a thousand clown suits.
A DRESSING ROOM.
And a check-out room. To select and check out
customs before the 10th.
PRIVATELY.
And on the 10th they come hidden in their dress.
PURPOSELY HID.
And they hide for 20 minutes.
FROM ONE ANOTHER.
Like clowns they hide.
And they are what they want to be.
DANCING LADIES AND HOBOS
AND ALL THE REST.
Wearing happy faces and sad ones
and young ones and angry ones.
AS THEY FEEL.
And they hide. For 20 minutes
on the night of the 10th they hide.
AND THEY HUNT ONE ANOTHER.
They hide and hunt
to see who the clown is.
WHO THE PERSON IS.
For 20 minutes they hide,
and then for 20 minutes they take off their masks.
AND LAUGH. AND THEY LAUGH.
At how they fooled one another.
AND WERE FOOLED.
And before the hour is done, they sing.
FOR TWENTY MINUTES THEY SING.
Easter songs.
THERE ARE MIRRORS ON ALL THE WALLS.
THEY SING AND SEE.
They cannot help laughing at one another.
AND AT THEMSELVES.
And because of the words of the songs.
IT WAS IN THE CIRCUS HE LEARNED
TO LAUGH AT HIMSELF.
AND TO BE LAUGHED AT.
Now on the 10th of each month
he helps others do it too.

*We are not alike.
Of this we need not be afraid.
Lord, remove this fear,
and give us the gift of laughing.
Making laughing at ourselves
an act of worship.
Christ, if You can laugh at death,
we can surely smile in life.
Amen.*

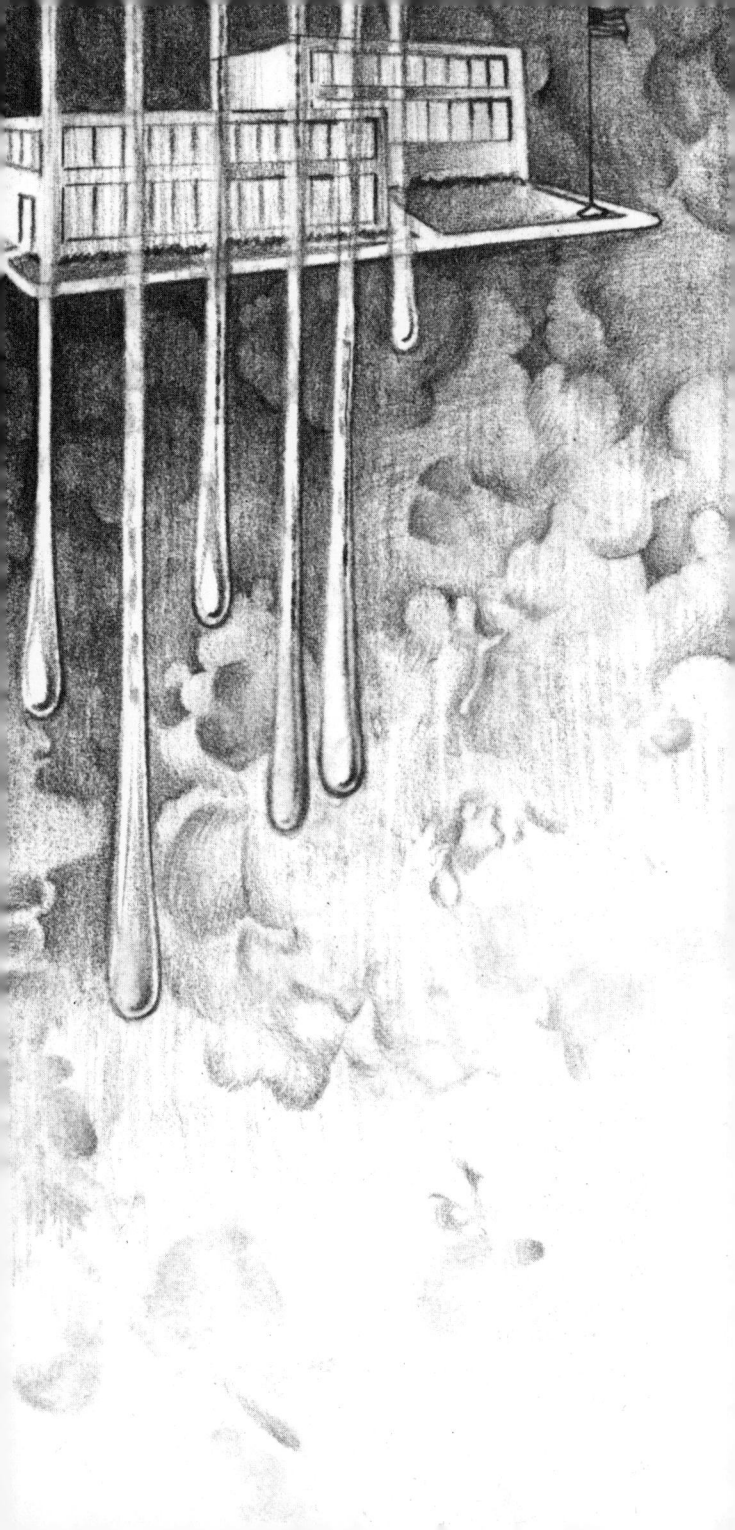

A School Cry

30 sat on the living-room floor.
They met with a playwright.
He asked them
what he should do next.
What did they want?
Where did they care?
They cried, "School!"

They had burst out,
spoken out,
and laughed out loud.
They had a good cry.
Now they could go back to school.
Things could be different.

Do a fantasy.
ON BECOMING A PERSON.
On changing your bottom
to fit the chair.
ON HAVING TO SIT IN GRANDPA'S CHAIR.
Hey. That could be a song.
That was grandpa's chair.
A SATIRE ON SCHOOL.
Call it "The School."
YEAH. SURE.
The school is its own satire.
THE YEARBOOK DOES A GOOD JOB.
Ha. Ha. Ha. Ha.
ON HITTING THE SYSTEM.
On graduation.
AND THE VALEDICTORIAN COULD
DO A CARTWHEEL.
Dress codes.
YEAH. HEA. WOW.
Lunch.
OH, NO. SURE.
Administration. Principals.
WOW.

The prom.
MARGIE AND BILL TAKE THAT ONE.
Cheerleading.
PHYLLIS AND DEB DO THAT.
Study halls.
THAT'S DEBBIE'S.
Teachers.
I'LL TAKE THAT.
Student morale.
OH, NO.
Let's make a list and write down feelings
and ideas and poems
and anything.
AND GATHER THEM LATER.
And give it a story line. A format.
LIKE AN UNDERGROUND NEWSPAPER.
A new kid in school.
A satire on the school.
WE'LL WRITE IT.
Produce it and give it.
WHY?
Why what?
WHAT'S THE REASON?
Maybe we'll find out.
LET'S JUST DO IT.
And maybe find out.
ABOUT THE SCHOOL.
How about, "I cried my first day in school"?
I CRIED MY LAST DAY IN SCHOOL.
Who's been sitting in my chair?
A SCHOOL CRY.
A cry.
YEAH.
A cry.
MY CRY.

It's a long way through school.
Many hours. Many years.
It's where a lot
of shaping takes place.
Keep me plastic. Keep me safe in the system.
Make me alive, Lord. I want to live a lot.
Amen.

She Needed a Question

It was a village in the Cascades.
A creative community, they said.
He was old. She was new.
She needed a beginning
and someone to ask
a new question.

Her poem was in a box.
None had heard it.
Then someone found it.
She sang and they applauded.
All in the same day.

She had it in a book.
A SCRAPBOOK.
Boxed in. In the middle.
BURIED IN ONE OF THE PAGES:
IN AN ENVELOPE.
The people had not seen it.
SHE HAD NOT WRITTEN IT THAT WAY.
IT WAS SCRAWLING AND IMPERFECT.
Corrections.
IT WAS IN HER HEAD FOR MANY DAYS.
Perhaps years. She did not know.
Now it was in the book.
The spiral book.
AND IT WAS UNDER THE THINGS.
STORED THERE.
She kept it there. Under them all.
BUT HE ASKED HER IF SHE WROTE.
She had waited longer
than the poem for this question.
AND HE ASKED HER HOW SHE FELT
WHEN SHE WROTE.
And what kind of pen and pencil she had.

AND WHAT SIDE OF THE PAGE
AND IF THERE WERE ANY MARGINS.
And why.
THEY HAD NOT ASKED HER SO MUCH.
And if there were any pictures with it.
AND SO THERE WASN'T ANYTHING
TO DO BUT SHOW HIM.
And let him read it.
AND SAY WHATEVER HE WOULD.
And take the chance of what he thought.
SHE SAID SHE WOULD LEAVE WHILE HE READ.
He asked her to stay.
HE TOOK THE CHANCE OF HER
BEING PRESENT WHEN HE READ IT.
And he laughed at the happy days
of Walter Wumple in the poem
and liked every letter.
AND EVERY LINE.
Plus the line she wrote
on the carbon copy to him.
THE LINE READ: "LET'S NEVER GROW UP."
And then she sang a song.
ABOUT A BALLOON LADY.
Blind. Holding balloons.
AND HE ASKED HER TO READ
TO THE MANY PEOPLE THAT NIGHT.
And to sing the song.
WITH HIM.
And with the other writers.
THE LINE EVERYONE LIKED BEST THAT NIGHT
WAS THE ONE ABOUT THE BALLOON LADY:
"I sell color and happiness
tied with a string."
HE LED THE PEOPLE IN APPLAUSE.
He still goes on writing.
SHE HAS BEGUN.
And he keeps asking who writes.

Lord,
there are so many
private poems and silent stories

waiting to be sung.
Waiting for the first reading.
Lord, in our midst
bring them out
into the light of day.
Amen.

FUNDERBURG LIBRARY

MANCHESTER COLLEGE

811.54 B787b
Brokering, Herbert, 1926-
Break out

DATE DUE

WITHDRAWN from Funderburg Library